Coaching and Mentoring in Higher Education

A learning-centred approach

Eileen Carnell, Jacqui MacDonald
and Susan Askew

Institute of Education
University of London

First published in 2006 by the Institute of Education, University of London,
20 Bedford Way, London WC1H 0AL

www.ioe.ac.uk/publications

British Library Cataloguing in Publication Data:
A catalogue record for this publication is available from the British Library

ISBN 0 85473 752 9

Eileen Carnell, Jacqui MacDonald and Susan Askew assert the moral right to be identified as the authors of this work.

Designed by Peter Dolton
Production services by Book Production Consultants Limited, Cambridge
Printed by The Burlington Press, Foxton, Cambridge

Contents

Acknowledgements

We would like to thank the following for their valuable comments on the draft document: Fiona Rodger, Sheila King, Nova Matthias, Duane Lai Fook, Katie Edwards, Rajna Patel, Rhoda Mukasa, Richard Palmer, Jo Biggs and Beatrice Peries. We are also grateful to Mark Tester for his help with layout.

1 Introduction

The purpose of this handbook is to present a clear organisational rationale for Higher Education coaching and mentoring schemes. It is based on a model developed at the Institute of Education, University of London.

Our purpose in writing the book is to promote coaching and mentoring in Higher Education (HE) as a way of enabling more effective working practices and to develop understanding of the concepts of coaching and mentoring and their underpinning rationales. We want to encourage constructivist learning-centred approaches that will enable coaching and mentoring to be as effective as possible.

At strategic points in the handbook we have included activities for self-reflection and/or group discussion. Each activity is also included as a photocopiable resource on the CD-ROM that accompanies this book.

ACTIVITY 1	• Briefly outline your experiences of being a coach/mentor and/or coachee/mentee.
	• Note any thoughts you have had about the process and any significant areas of learning.

2 *Coaching and mentoring: definitions and models*

This chapter examines some definitions and models of coaching and mentoring, analyses the concepts and principles that underpin them and considers their links with conceptions of learning.

It is often helpful to trace terms from their origins to understand their meaning and the concepts on which they are based. The term coach can be traced to the apprenticeship system, where an older, more experienced worker passed down his or her job skills and knowledge to the younger generation. It has been described as a 'process that enhances the development and performance of individuals and teams' (Arnot and Sparrow, 2004: 6). Today the term is often used in a sporting context but is becoming more widespread in industry and education. A recent research study indicates that the provision of external coaching services across the UK has soared over the last few years (Arnot and Sparrow, 2004: 1).

Mentoring has its roots in the writings of Homer. Mentor was an older, wiser man who was asked by Odysseus, the king of Ithaca, to look after his son when he went to fight in the Trojan War. The role of Mentor was not just to care for his charge but to prepare him for the responsibilities and tasks ahead (Rogers, 2004: 23). Today the term mentor has become synonymous with the concept of trusted adviser, a more experienced and more knowledgeable colleague, usually in the same organisation or linked with the organisation, who is not a line manager but a 'career friend' (Rogers, 2004: 23). This person acts as a guide and supporter.

There are many definitions of coaching and mentoring. Table 1 examines four and draws out the concepts that underpin them.

TABLE 1

Some definitions of
coaching and mentoring
and their underpinning
concepts

- Decide which of the definitions in Table 1 most appeals to you. Indicate your reasons. How does that definition connect with your own experiences?

- What issues/areas do you think are missing from these definitions?

TABLE 1 Some definitions of coaching and mentoring and their underpinning concepts

Coaching	Mentoring
Definitions The coach works with clients to achieve speedy, increased and sustainable effectiveness in their lives and careers through focused learning. The coach's sole aim is to work with the client to achieve all of the client's potential – as defined by the client. (Rogers, 2004)	A mentor is an experienced and trusted adviser, normally a teacher or leader with experience of the role or organisation. In education, the role is commonly associated with both professional and personal responsibilities. A mentor may offer expertise and professional wisdom on pedagogical or leadership matters, providing support in the development of new skills, whilst also advising on concerns about general welfare and career choices. (Cordingly *et al.*, 2004)
A specialist coach offers expertise to help review and develop established practice or integrate new ways of doing things. (Cordingly *et al.*, 2004).	Mentoring is a relationship between two parties, who are not connected within a line management structure, in which one party (the mentor) guides the other (the mentee) through a period of change and towards an agreed objective. (Kay and Hinds, 2005)
Underpinning concepts and principles The coach is more knowledgeable and expert in the particular innovation or approach and will offer support for implementation and evaluation of the new practice. (Cordingly *et al.*, 2004)	A mentor is seen as being an equal and is supportive of the changes that the mentee wishes to make in a trusting and confidential relationship. (Kay and Hinds, 2005)
The client is resourceful; the coach's role is to encourage the client's resourcefulness; the process addresses the whole person; the client sets the agenda; both coach and coachee are equals; the process is about change and action. (Rogers, 2004)	A mentor supports an individual as s/he experiences shifts in professional identity, taking an active role in defining the learning agenda at the start of the relationship in the light of their additional knowledge and experience, but gradually enabling the mentee to take an increasingly active role in shaping their own learning. A mentor, drawing on the expertise of a range of colleagues (e.g. subject specialists), will act as a broker and communication channel to construct a coherent learning programme for the Mentee. (Cordingly *et al.*, 2004).

2.2 DIFFERENCES BETWEEN COACHING AND MENTORING

TABLE 2

Differences between coaching and mentoring

These definitions indicate some overlap and some differences between coaching and mentoring. Mentoring is often seen as a longer-term process, for example offering support during a career change such as becoming a senior manager. In her book *Transformational Mentoring* Hay (1995) describes mentoring as a 'developmental alliance'; a relationship between equals in which someone is helped to develop themselves. Coaching may be shorter-term and more focused, for example offering support for academic writing. Table 2 makes this distinction explicit.

Coaching is normally used to support the process of reviewing established or emerging practice. It is focused on innovation, change or specific skills (Cordingly *et al.*, 2004).	**Mentoring** is usually concerned with supporting practitioners whilst they make a significant career transition, for example with becoming a teacher or school leader. (Cordingly *et al.*, 2004)
Coaching is conceived as a more structured learning process aimed at explicit professional development in an agreed area(s) of performance. (Pennington, 2004)	**Mentoring** is intended to be supportive of the individual and occurs 'at need'. Here the emphasis is on ready and confidential access to a 'critical friend' who can be used as a sounding board and who offers a 'free' form of advice. (Pennington, 2004)

FIGURE 1 Activities involved in coaching and mentoring and their overlap

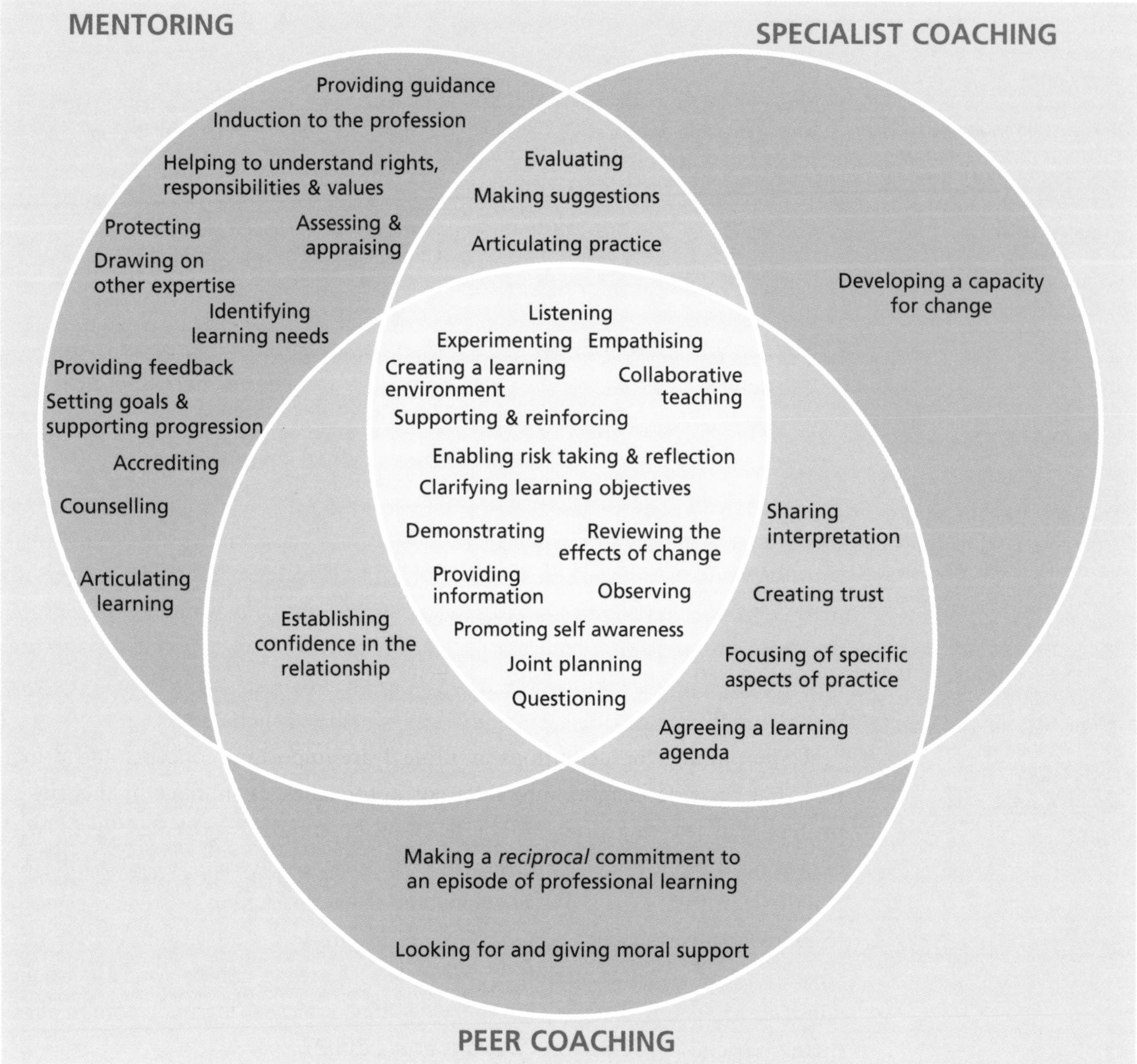

MENTORING

SPECIALIST COACHING

Providing guidance

Induction to the profession

Helping to understand rights, responsibilities & values

Evaluating

Making suggestions

Protecting

Assessing & appraising

Articulating practice

Drawing on other expertise

Identifying learning needs

Developing a capacity for change

Providing feedback

Setting goals & supporting progression

Accrediting

Counselling

Articulating learning

Listening

Experimenting Empathising

Creating a learning environment

Collaborative teaching

Supporting & reinforcing

Enabling risk taking & reflection

Clarifying learning objectives

Demonstrating Reviewing the effects of change

Sharing interpretation

Providing information Observing

Creating trust

Establishing confidence in the relationship

Promoting self awareness

Joint planning

Focusing of specific aspects of practice

Questioning

Agreeing a learning agenda

Making a *reciprocal* commitment to an episode of professional learning

Looking for and giving moral support

PEER COACHING

Source: Cordingly *et al.*, 2004

Coaching tends to be seen as one aspect of mentoring; mentoring may include coaching (Bush *et al.*, 1996) or is one of the core skills of mentoring (Clutterbuck, 1992). The overlap in activities is illustrated in Figure 1.

Creating a learning environment is central in this diagram; this is a key feature in both coaching and mentoring. Alongside this are activities that suggest learning activities, for example, enabling risk taking and reflection, experimenting and clarifying learning objectives. The specialist coaching section differs in that this is devoted to developing a capacity for change, whereas in the mentoring section the nearest to this idea is setting goals and supporting progression and articulating learning.

What is striking here is that coaching is seen as bringing about change, whereas in mentoring this is not explicit. This calls into question the views of learning underpinning this diagram and what models of learning are being suggested. Views of learning tell us about different conceptions of learning and models of learning about the different ways in which learning comes about.

<table>
<tr><td>ACTIVITY 3</td><td>

• Think about the differences between coaching and mentoring in relation to your own experiences.

• In what ways do you find the definitions of coaching and mentoring used here connect with your practices and what you imagine your practices might be in the future?

• If you favour one approach more than another, indicate your reasons.

• What areas/issues might be missing?

• How do you think your own and other people's different purposes might determine whether a coaching or mentoring approach is more appropriate?

</td></tr>
</table>

2.3 COACHING AND MENTORING AND LINKS WITH LEARNING

Interpretations of coaching and mentoring differ. For example, the perception of learning that the coach or mentor holds will affect their stance. It is often not made clear in literature on coaching and mentoring which models of learning underpin different approaches: that is, how learning comes about. It is important that the underpinning model of learning, view of the learner (coachee, mentee) and view of the learning process is made explicit.

Underpinning the definitions in Table 1 are important concepts and principles that provide insights into different approaches. A number of theories of professional learning point to the learning potential of working closely with experienced practitioners (Hobson, 2003). Some argue that 'real life skills' are usually learnt with the aid of coaching and that feedback on practice is essential to skills acquisition (Sloboda, 1986 cited in Hobson, 2003). Support for construction and co-construction approaches to learning can be found in social-cultural perspectives based on the view that effective learning comes about through social participation (Watkins *et al.*, 2002).

Three models are used to examine the way learning may come about in coaching and mentoring: instruction, construction and co-construction (developed from Watkins *et al.* 2002).

The instruction model (learning by teaching)

The instruction model is dominant for adults and young people in universities and schools, yet it is critised for being less effective for learning (Watkins *et al.*, 2002). It is also considered less effective for coaching and mentoring (Rogers, 2004). If learning is seen from this perspective then coaching or mentoring is likely to:

• focus on teaching more than learning
  ○ the coach/mentor gives advice to the coachee/mentee
  ○ the mentor does more of the talking
  ○ the mentor is seen as 'expert'
• include talk about learning in ways that conflate learning with performance
  the coach/mentor might ask the coachee/mentee to talk about what they want to achieve rather than what they want to learn

- value concrete products, which are easily measurable
- de-emphasise the process of learning
- de-emphasise social dimensions of learning.

The construction models (construction and co-construction) are less common and yet far more effective for coaching and mentoring.

The construction model (learning by understanding)

If learning is seen from this perspective then mentoring or coaching is likely to:
- focus on learning more than teaching
  - it supports the coachee's/mentee's understanding
  - the mentor will do less of the talking and is seen as 'a facilitator'
- focus on the way the coachee/mentee make sense of their experiences
- address thought-demanding questions and value processes which make learning visible
- ask of every process: 'What can we learn from this?'

The co-construction model (learning through dialogue)

If learning is seen from this perspective then coaching or mentoring is likely to:
- focus on learning more than teaching
  - reaching joint understanding through dialogue
  - the coach/mentor will do less of the talking and is seen as a 'co-coachee'/ 'co-mentee'
- focus on social and collaborative processes
- see the process as building knowledge and learning through dialogue
- value processes which enhance collaborative outcomes
- seek to improve learning by enhancing collaborative enquiry.

ACTIVITY 4

- In what ways have the description of these models of learning extended your understanding of the process of coaching and mentoring?

- What, if anything, do you think is missing?

- Is there an alternative way of looking at the connections between coaching/ mentoring and learning? If so, explain.

2.4 COACHING AND MENTORING AND LINKS WITH EFFECTIVE LEARNING

Constructivist approaches are more likely to support effective learning in coaching and mentoring, but there are limitations with the instruction model. For example, a problem with giving advice is that it can lead to the coachee/mentee becoming dependent on the coach or mentor. The coachee/mentee in this approach is seen as passive whereas, in the definition provided by Jenny Rogers (see Table 1), he or she is seen as resourceful and active. Rogers suggests that the process is about drawing out intrinsic human resourcefulness.

It follows that if the coach/mentor views the learner (coachee/mentee) as active and resourceful the coach/mentor will have to find alternatives to giving advice (Rogers, 2004: 30). Constructivist approaches do exactly this: the coachee/mentee is seen as active in learning; resourceful and responsible for learning.

From our own survey of the writing coach scheme at the Institute of Education (see Appendix 1) our writing coaches often find that it is enough to listen and to give space to talk about the writing. Through speaking aloud about what they are trying to say the coachee's ideas are clarified. They hear what it is they need to write. The coach acts as a facilitator. In this way the coachee takes ownership of the process and subsequent action. It is striking that the participants in this study valued the focus on their individual needs and the way in which they came to understand their own learning. This resulted in a changed view of themselves as writers.

Pennington's study for HESDA (2004) found that senior managers in higher education learn more effectively when, for example:

- high levels of challenge coexist with personal support for the learner
- individual learning is integrated with group and organisational learning
- an appropriate balance is struck between knowledge/understanding, reflection and action
- a variety of formal and informal means are used to promote learning.

The HESDA study shows that new professional development initiatives based on this approach would be well received.

An analysis of our own survey and HESDA's research indicates that in effective learning approaches in higher education attention is given to:

- the learner (the personal dimension)
- the learning (the transformational dimension)
- the learning context (the organisational and social dimension)
- and learning about learning (the meta-learning dimension).

These four dimensions can be the focus of a learning conversation in coaching/mentoring.

The learner (the personal dimension)

In learning-centred approaches the role of the learner (coachee/mentee) is made explicit. The emphasis is on the coachee's/mentee's own learning and is designed to have an effect on them as a professional – teacher, researcher, writer, or leader/manager. If teachers, for example, are more aware of their own learning and what helps or hinders it, they are more able to support the learning of their students. Professionals who have more sophisticated conceptions of learning are more likely to adopt 'higher level' approaches in the classroom (Trigwell and Prosser, 1996). If writers are more aware of their own writing processes and what helps and hinders their writing then they are more likely both to become more confident writers and are able to support others in their writing too. The same principles apply to leaders and managers.

The coach/mentor needs to be aware of the ways in which coachees/mentees can focus on themselves as learners. This can be the focus of the review stage of the learning conversation (see p. 8).

The learning (the transformational dimension)

In coaching and mentoring transformation or change comes about through the learning conversation. The conversation enables the process of coaching/mentoring in which there needs to be an explicit focus on learning. Dennison and Kirk's cycle of learning (1990) is useful for this purpose.

FIGURE 2

The learning cycle

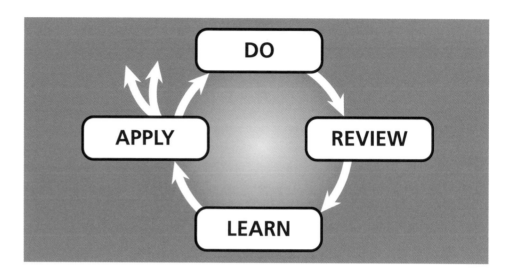

Developed from Kolb (1984), this cycle outlines an explicit process of reflecting, analysing, evaluating, making connections and planning action for change. This cycle highlights activity in learning (Do), the need for reflection and evaluation (Review) the extraction of meaning from this review (Learn) and the planned use of learning in future action (Apply). This cycle in practice is complex and dynamic allowing professionals to determine the changes they wish to make.

Prompts for a learning conversation based on this cycle can be found in Appendix 2. The necessary skills are highlighted. They include: the ability to build rapport; active listening, observing and interpreting and helping others learn.

The learning context (the organisational and social dimension)

A learning-centred model highlights the importance of the learning context in which the coachee/mentee is working. This matches with Little's view on becoming a better teacher: 'Imagine that you would become a better teacher, just by virtue of being on the staff of a particular school – just from that one fact alone' (Little, 1990). Some environments are more supportive than others and the factors that help or hinder mentee's and coachee's learning can be usefully discussed.

The coach or mentor can help the coachee/mentee focus on understanding the possibilities and constraints inside the organisation by reflection, identification of new insights, and then on the action that the individual may wish to take.

Learning about learning (the meta-learning dimension)

Participants in a learning-centred model are encouraged to reflect on their own learning, because learning is complex and can be disturbing and frustrating as well as exciting. The use of the Dennison and Kirk's learning circle (1990) (Figure 2) at a meta-learning level is demonstrated in the learning conversation in Appendix 2. In this case professionals are made aware explicitly of their own learning – meta-learning. The learning conversation (Appendix 2) is designed to draw attention to this dimension.

Figure 3 usefully distinguishes learning and meta-learning as do the following definitions:

> *Learning is the process of creating knowledge by making sense of experience....*
> *Meta-learning is the process of making sense of your experience of learning.*

(Watkins *et al.*, 1998: 21)

FIGURE 3

The meta-learning cycle

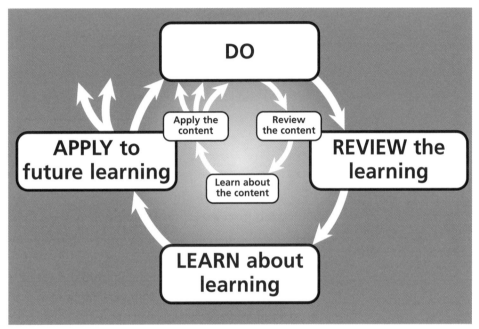

Source: Watkins, 2001

Meta-learning makes sense of individual's learning experiences by, for example, making the emotional responses explicit and examining how behaviour and relationships affect learning.

ACTIVITY 5	• These dimensions of learning are presented to reflect the complexity of the process of coaching and mentoring. In what ways do you think these dimensions might inform your practice? • There may be some areas of complexity that are missing. What occurs to you that would add important insights?

2.5 WHAT COACHING AND MENTORING IS NOT

Coaching and mentoring is not counselling, although some counselling skills may be used by the coach/mentor. Learning conversations do not focus on personal problems. If people need counselling then the organisation should provide this separately or refer them to an appropriate professional.

Neither is the learning conversation therapy, although the outcome of the conversation may leave the person feeling up-lifted and that their emotions have changed. But learning is always the focus.

3 *Benefits of coaching and mentoring*

Because the process of coaching and mentoring is carried out in the workplace, as part of everyday activities, it may be both more effective and less time-consuming than other forms of professional development. It is a very effective way of using time because it relates to the individual's needs and may be the most powerful and cost-effective form of professional learning.

3.1
BENEFITS TO THE COACHEE/MENTEE

For many years mentoring has been associated with a wide range of benefits, from career advancement and heightened self-confidence to an increased sense of belonging (Hansford *et al*. 2002 cited in Hobson, 2003).

From our own staff survey of two schemes already operating at the Institute of Education with writing coaches and peer mentoring groups (see Appendix 1) the following benefits emerge:

Having a writing coach helps an individual to:
- reflect
- feel less isolated
- share new understandings with other colleagues
- seek help from others
- have more confidence
- be more aware of the writing process
- reassess issues
- develop individual skills as a writer.

Being part of a peer mentoring group helps individuals to:
- think about goals and how to achieve them
- articulate issues in a conscious and thoughtful way
- feel less isolated
- gain a perspective on issues and concerns
- see ways through difficulties
- review and make sense of feelings
- feel uplifted
- deal with difficulties.

Mentoring for senior managers

In the evaluation of a pilot project of the national mentoring scheme for senior managers in higher education it was found that participants gained:
- insight into high-level leadership issues and processes

- understanding of how HE is different from other contexts
- opportunities to look at familiar issues from an unfamiliar angle
- increased confidence in facing difficult situations.

One participant said: 'I have learned to value my analytical skills. I am more confident in my value to an organisation and prepared to negotiate the conditions necessary for me to be working at peak performance' (Pennington, 2004). This last comment indicates a positive transformation as a result of the mentoring process.

Other research also indicates high levels of satisfaction: Bolam *et al.* (1993) found 66 per cent of new head teachers and 73 per cent of mentors rated the process of the headteacher mentoring pilot scheme as successful or very successful. Grover (1994), involved in a similar scheme in the United States, found 80 per cent stated that mentoring had been helpful or extremely helpful. Arnot and Sparrow (2004: 31) found that although current practice is variable there is clear evidence that a more systematic and structured approach to the use of coaching will contribute greater value: 'Coaching works but it could be better; there is a growing awareness and appreciation of the value of Coaching and at the same time a recognition of its limitations'.

In the evaluation of a pilot project of the national mentoring scheme for senior managers in higher education it was found that 95 per cent of mentees graded their mentoring sessions highly for being productive, stimulating and supportive; 90 per cent would encourage other senior colleagues to participate in a similar process; 81 per cent of mentees believed that participating in the scheme had directly enhanced their expertise as managers and supported the development of management/leadership skills (Pennington, 2004).

3.2 BENEFITS TO THE COACH/MENTOR

Mentors and coaches experience gains in:
- enhanced professional development; new skills and areas of expertise are developed
- updated knowledge and ideas
- insights and understandings through supervision
- increased peer recognition
- increased personal reputation
- increased job satisfaction.
  (Kay and Hinds, 2005)

- benefits to own professional development
- improved performance/problem analysis
- insights into current practice
- awareness of different approaches to coaching and mentoring
- increased reflectiveness
- improved self-esteem.
  (Hobson, 2003)

In the evaluation of a pilot project of the national mentoring scheme for senior managers in higher education it was found that mentors considered the process to be part of their own professional development (Pennington, 2004). Cordingly *et al.* (2004) concur: being a mentor or a coach is itself a rich source of professional development in which the process of making tacit knowledge and expertise visible and explicit for a colleague creates an opportunity for reflection and learning for both.

3.3

BENEFITS TO THE ORGANISATION

It follows that positive effects for the organisation can accrue. Douglas's (1997) review found a range of benefits from the organisation's perspective:

- increased productivity and motivation
- improved recruitment
- increased organisational communication
- improved succession planning
- management development
- reduced staff turnover
- increased organisational commitment
- strengthening and continuance of corporate culture.

There is a need to be cautious, however. Daresh (1995) suggests that there has been a remarkable lack of systematic analysis of the benefits of coaching and mentoring in the research literature.

The results of our own survey (see Appendix 1) suggest that working collaboratively, being open, trusting, challenging, taking risks and celebrating success make work-related learning more effective in bringing about learning and change than some other forms of professional development. These results suggest development of a professional learning community where all members of the organisation are in a process of review, reflection and improvement (Louis and Kruse, 1995).

Policy development

HE establishments need to ensure there is congruence across policy documents. Where coaching/mentoring is introduced, the documents need to be congruent with existing teaching and learning policies.

ACTIVITY 6

- In your experience, which would you say were the most important benefits to:

  (a) the coachee/mentee

  (b) the coach/mentor

  (c) the organisation

- Are there any other benefits that you can identify?

4 The roles of the coach and coachee, mentor and mentee

It is crucial that the roles of the coach and coachee, mentor and mentee are clarified – especially at the start of the process.

4.1
STARTING THE PROCESS

On the first occasion that the coach/mentor meets the coachee/mentee it is important to establish the purpose of the meetings and to share an understanding of the nature of the process. It is helpful to be explicit about this. This chapter and Appendices 2 and 3 provide information about preparing for the first meeting.

During the conversation the roles of the coach/mentor and coachee/mentee are outlined. If the expectations of both are discussed at this early stage this will prevent misunderstandings developing later. The coachee/mentee needs to be clear about their objectives. It may be useful for them to have a copy of section 4.3, 'The role of the coachee/mentee', (a photocopiable version is included in the CD-ROM). The emphasis needs to be on how the coach/mentor helps the coachee/mentee through a process rather than doing the work for them (Kay and Hinds, 2005). It may be useful to distinguish between the role of the coach/mentor and relationships that the coachee/mentee has with other colleagues, for example their line manager.

4.2
THE ROLE OF THE COACH/MENTOR

The following suggestions may be helpful for a person new to the role of coach/mentor (this list is included in the photocopiable resources in the CD-ROM):

- Introduce yourself to the mentee/coachee as soon as possible after accepting the role and set the date for the first meeting.

- Encourage the mentee/coachee to think about what they want from the process.

- Clarify that the process is about ensuring that their needs are the focus and your role is to support them in achieving their aims.

- Stress that confidentiality is of utmost importance.

- Discuss the best place and time to meet to suit their interests.

- Make regular contact; if you are making another appointment leave sufficient time to do so before the meeting ends. It might be more appropriate to book a series of meetings in advance. If the coachee/mentee cancels an appointment make another appointment straight away. Do not let the process drift.

- If the coachee/mentee does not attend the appointment and does not contact you, contact them to offer another appointment.

- Encourage the coachee/mentee to think about the way that the process is suiting their needs: check from time to time that the approach is still appropriate.

- Be clear about the boundaries of the relationship: keep a professional distance. Be prepared for an invitation to meet socially and decide what your response might be. This might be to celebrate success.

- At the start of each meeting ensure that the coachee's/mentee's agenda has been clarified. For example, a session could start with the question 'What do you want from the meeting today?'

- Keep to the start and finishing times of meetings. Towards the end of the meeting you might want to remind the mentee/coachee how much time there is left. Ask whether the mentee/coachee has covered the ground they wanted to in the session.

- Build in a review, especially if you are coming towards the end of a block of sessions.

- Talk to the coachee/mentee at an appropriate point about the ending of a block of sessions. This may be at the end of a particular event, for example, at the end of the probationary period or for the completion of a specific project. The ending needs to be explicit and appropriate and a discussion of what, if anything, might replace the relationship needs to be discussed.
  (Developed from Kay and Hinds, 2005)

4.3

THE ROLE OF THE COACHEE/MENTEE

The role of the coachee/mentee is to ensure that their professional needs are being met in the meetings. They should think about what they need from the meetings and make this clear to the coach/mentor. They need to:

- take responsibility for their learning

- consider and articulate their agenda for each meeting

- make it clear how the sessions are meeting their needs and whether the approach taken by the coach/mentor is appropriate. They have to make this clear; the coach/mentor cannot guess what the coachee/mentee is thinking

- take a note of any action that has been decided. It is not up to the coach/mentor to do this

- be as honest as they can about how they understand the issues being discussed and their responsibility to it

- honour the meetings arranged and be on time; if they have to change a meeting time they need to record the next date in their diary and keep it, even if things are going well

- stick to the agenda and not stray into other areas

- be clear about the boundaries of the relationship: keep a professional distance

- regard all conversations as confidential

- be realistic and not expect the coach/mentor to solve their problems

- ensure that the coach/mentor has any tasks to read in advance of the next meeting. For example a writing coach may require new writing some time before the next meeting. They need to make sure when the coach needs this material and stick to the time agreed, even if the writing is not complete. (Developed from Kay and Hinds, 2005)

4.4 THE ROLE OF THE CONVERSATION

The key role for the coach/mentor is to facilitate the conversation. The most important role is to listen to what the person has to say and to move them forward in their learning and achieve what they have identified as their objectives. A model has been developed to encourage this structure (see Appendix 2). In this model questions or prompts take the person further in their thinking by reviewing the situation (for example, the writing they have produced), identifying new insights and understanding and identifying next steps. If the person has been active and responsible in the conversation they are more likely to become more effective and often more confident in their approach.

Effective questions

Some effective questions have been identified by Rogers (2004: 65). Examples of specific questions are contained in Appendix 3.

The characteristics of effective questions are that they:

- raise the person's self-awareness by provoking thinking and challenge
- demand truthful answers by cutting through obfuscation and waffle
- are short
- go beyond asking for information by asking for discovery
- encourage the person to take responsibility
- stick to the agenda
- lead to learning
- are 'open' in that they cannot be answered by a 'yes' or 'no' response.

The role of the coach or mentor is to help the person make their agenda explicit. In the learning-centred process it is the coachee/mentee who identifies the issues that are important for them to discuss. Hence the question at the start of the session, 'What is it you would like to get from today's meeting? ' This provides a purpose and agenda for the meeting. The mentor or coach does not have an agenda.

A useful point to consider is how the focus of the meetings may change over time: 'Progressive focusing tends to occur through time and the longer the duration of the relationship, the more the parties involved tend to feel the need to define why they are meeting and what the looked for outcomes might be' (Pennington, 2004).

Within the learning-centred approach the role of the coach or mentor is to help the person become more effective in what they do.

| ACTIVITY 7 | • In what ways would you say that Chapter 4 has helped you clarify the different roles? |
| | • What issues does this chapter raise for you? |

5 What helps or hinders the process of coaching and mentoring?

This section draws on research studies to highlight what participants have identified as factors that help or hinder effective coaching and mentoring schemes.

5.1 WHAT HELPS EFFECTIVE COACHING AND MENTORING?

The research review carried out by Pennington (2004) indicates that:

- Mentoring is more effective when it is formalised and when the expectations and commitments of participants are made explicit.

- The quality of the mentoring process is enhanced when participants are provided with guidelines and/or training on effective practice and the management of the relationship.

- Mentors drawn from outside the organisation are generally at least as effective as those from within and in some circumstances may provide added benefit.

- Mentoring works equally well in pairings of mixed gender or race as it does with same gender or race pairings.

- The mentoring process is strengthened when care is taken to match individuals in terms of needs, geographical location and personal preferences.

- Given the centrality of confidentiality and trust in the mentoring process, it is important to design ground rules for the management of significant ethical issues at the earliest possible point in the relationship.

- Mentoring is particularly effective when individuals are new to a role, engage in major career transitions or work in environments where change is frequent.

Effective relationships in a learning-centred approach

In a learning-centered approach the relationship is non-hierarchical. It is most important that coaching or mentoring takes place outside the line management relationship. The relationship needs to be based on mutual respect in a non-judgmental atmosphere. This is important for the development of trust.

There is no single model; the approach needs to be appropriate for the specific circumstances, but some basic principles apply to any situation:

- The mentor or coach needs to be independent.

- The purpose of the process needs to be agreed.

- The means of contact needs to be agreed and reviewed.

- Confidentiality needs to be maintained.
  (Kay and Hinds, 2005)

Necessary personal qualities and skills in a learning-centred approach

Certain qualities are important in a coach/mentor. These include enthusiasm, commitment, willingness and approachability (Kay and Hinds, 2005). Openness, trust, respect, tolerance, honesty, integrity, support and encouragement are also important (Pennington, 2004). Discretion is vital, as is a sense of humour. The following qualities are also desirable: a wish to see others succeed, empathy, sensitivity, patience, a willingness to make time for people and confidence in what can and cannot be done. Having an appreciative outlook can support the individual to achieve whatever they believe is achievable.

Important skills in a coach/mentor include: listening skills (genuine listening is about acceptance); rapport and congruence (real rapport comes from unconditional acceptance of the other person); developing a non-threatening atmosphere; and the ability to focus on the other person's agenda (developed from Rogers, 2004: 42–3).

Other forms of contact

While face-to-face meetings are most helpful, contact does not always have to be in this form. Sometimes the use of email and phone calls between meetings is helpful provided both are happy with these arrangements.

Professional ethics and confidentiality

Ethical guidelines need to inform coaching and mentoring practices.

Sharon Gewirtz (2004) presents a set of ethical issues in relation to research. This approach she calls ethical reflexivity. Her ideas have been adapted here to inform these coaching and mentoring guidelines. For example, there is a need to:

- be explicit about the value assumptions and evaluative judgements that inform or are embedded in our practices
- be prepared to offer a defense of those assumptions and judgements to the extent that they might not be shared by others
- acknowledge tensions between the various values that are embedded in practice
- take seriously the practical judgements and dilemmas of the people that we are working with
- take responsibility for the political and ethical implications of our practice.

It is important to consider these ideas in relation to coaching and mentoring practices. For example, Sharon Gewirtz's ideas may have implications for the following:

- The way in which individuals seek support from the service and how information is shared with coaches/mentors. How are individuals who use the service protected?

- The 'matching' of mentees and coachees with mentors and coaches.

- The issues of confidentiality. What does this really mean? Do people share the same understanding of it? How important is it? How can confidentiality be maintained?

- Dual relationships in the workplace – for example the coach or mentor may work alongside a work colleague who is a coachee/mentee. What tensions might arise?

- The process of giving feedback. Who owns the knowledge, and how is it recorded and protected?

- Any conflict of values between coaching and mentoring practices and the wider institutional and work culture and the micro-politics of the mentee's/coachee's school, research unit, or department.

- There may also be issues of accountability. How can the coaches/mentors give an account of the work without breaking confidentiality? How are the coaches/mentors protected?

All these issues need to be included within the training courses for mentors and coaches and returned to during supervision sessions. Any tensions that the mentor or coach may face need to be discussed with the supervisor during supervision sessions.

5.2 WHAT HINDERS EFFECTIVE MENTORING OR COACHING?

The skills of coaching and mentoring are hard to acquire and evaluate but crucial to success (Cordingly *et al.*, 2004). Cordingly *et al.* warn that poor coaching and mentoring are often worse than no professional development at all because the process can build dependence or destroy confidence. In order to combat this risk many organisations put in place frameworks such as formal learning agreements to inhibit poor practice and scaffold good practice.

There are some specific issues that hinder effective coaching and mentoring:

- There are misunderstandings on either or both sides about the roles, obligations and expectations.

- The process is not a priority for either or both.

- The coachee and coach (mentor and mentee) do not respect each other.

- The coachee/mentee sees the process as an organisational requirement and does not enter the process with a wish to learn.

- The coach/mentor has been coerced into taking on the role and has little interest in the process.

- The coach/mentor does not see the process as an opportunity for learning but as a way of passing on his/her expertise or is patronising. (Developed from Rogers, 2004: 24)

This last point illustrates that the coach/mentor holds an instruction view of learning where the coachee/mentee is dependent and passive rather than the construction view where the coachee/mentee is resourceful and active.

When the process is not working

It is essential for the coach/mentor and coachee/mentee to review the process at regular intervals. This may help identify where the process might not be helpful. The coach/mentor may suggest to the mentee/coachee that an alternative coach/mentor be found. The service manager should be approached to arrange this.

ACTIVITY 8

- Now that you have read Chapter 5, list any concerns that you would like to discuss with your supervisor or colleagues in a workshop on coaching/mentoring.

A case study of coaching and mentoring: a programme of staff development and support networks at the Institute of Education, University of London

Informal networks of support have always existed in higher education. What is new at the Institute of Education is the focus on making the support networks explicit. A pilot scheme was set up to examine the extent to which such support could be an entitlement for all staff.

In the evaluation of a pilot project of the national mentoring scheme for senior managers in higher education it was found that there is a need to increase the volume and range of professional development activities for senior managers including coaching and mentoring (Pennington, 2004).

6.1
THE INTRODUCTION OF COACHING AND MENTORING AT THE INSTITUTE OF EDUCATION

From September 2005 the Institute of Education introduced the following scheme of coaching and mentoring.

1. A team of coaches/mentors was identified, representing both academic and non-academic staff. This team attended a three-day staff development course on coaching and mentoring run by colleagues. As part of the course the team examined and analysed a draft of this handbook and changes were made to it as a result of the feedback.

2. In addition to the three-day course, the coaches/mentors met for formal supervision and training sessions on a monthly basis. The supervisors were drawn from Institute of Education staff and were experienced coaches/mentors.

3. The staff development team advertised the support available across the Institute and was responsible for pairing the coachees/mentees with coaches/mentors. The staff development team facilitated the process.

4. The coaches/mentors then supported the staff development team in responding to specific requests on a one-to-one basis.

Issues to be considered in the evaluation of the coaching/mentoring scheme	Hobson (2003) reports that a range of factors is likely to have an impact on the effectiveness of mentoring: • the pairing of mentors/mentees • the qualities/attributes of the coach/mentor • whether or not the mentor has had training, and the quality of that training • the availability of time.

Elsewhere, other factors are highlighted: a structured approach, coaching qualifications and the 'right' personal style (Arnot and Sparrow, 2004: 2).

Lack of time is reported to be a key constant in a number of mentoring schemes (Hobson, 2003). Ways round the obstacle are considered. For example, the number of people the coach or mentor sees needs to be considered carefully and recognition of the time allowance should be made explicit.

Pairing is critical to the process. Arnot and Sparrow (2004) suggest that the criteria for the pairing process needs to be explicit. These may include the preferences of the coachee/mentee for a person of the same sex. As far as possible the preferences of coachees/mentees should be taken into account.

These issues inform the evaluation process (see Appendices 4 and 5) that we have developed at the Institute of Education.

The selection of mentors and coaches	Many different criteria apply in the selection of coaches, of which the most significant are: • coaching and mentoring experience • track record • personal style • cultural fit • a structured approach on the part of the coach. (adapted from Arnot and Sparrow, 2004: 2)

6.2
HOW THE PROCESS OPERATES

Step 1	Following requests to the staff development team the individual seeking coaching or mentoring is asked to identify what they see as the purpose of the coaching/mentoring, how they think they will benefit and their preferences for a coach/mentor (see Appendix 5).
Step 2	The staff development team locates a coach/mentor and an initial meeting is arranged by the coach/mentor (see page 13 for notes about the initial meeting).
Step 3	If the coach/mentor and coachee/mentee agree to go ahead a specific number of sessions is agreed (for example six sessions of coaching on a specific theme). Frequency and timing of meetings will be dependent on the context

and nature of the work to be done and will be negotiated according to needs and circumstances. If for some reason they do not think it is appropriate to work together the coachee/mentee will approach the staff development team and the pairing process will start again.

Step 4

The coach/mentor and coachee/mentee agree a way of working together (see pages 13–15).

Step 5

The coach/mentor and coachee/mentee agree to defend time for meetings. Dates and times are a priority in diaries for both parties.

Keeping notes

The purpose of keeping notes of the conversation is to remind the coachee/mentee what new insights or understandings they may have gained, what decisions they may have made and what actions they will take. These will be kept by the coachee/mentee and there is no need for the coach/mentor to keep a record.

How the notes are to be made is a matter for discussion between the coach/mentor and coachee/mentee. If the coach/mentor makes the notes during the session then they can hand them over to the coachee/mentee at the end or both parties may wish to draw up some notes at the end which the coachee/mentee then takes away.

Supervision for coaches/mentors

The coach/mentor meets a supervisor on a regular basis to discuss the issues that have arisen in their practice. The sessions will be run by supervisors and will be organised by the staff development team. Supervision is a process that encourages learning both individually and collectively and ensures high levels of consistency and effectiveness across the organisation.

6.3 COACHING AND MENTORING FOR SPECIFIC PHASES AND FOCI

Mentoring may be helpful for staff new to the organisation. Starting a new role may be a daunting experience and the support of a mentor can help people settle into their new working and learning context, and become familiar with the new culture during the period of probation. The Pennington (2004) study found that mentoring is particularly effective when individuals are being inducted to a new role, when they engage with major career transitions or when they work in environments subjected to widespread organisational change. Those who have been in post for a while may lack confidence and not see their true potential. There may be some who want to improve their skills and others who are looking to advance their career. All of these groups may benefit from mentoring.

Coaching may be helpful for the development of specific skills, for example in developing writing skills, understanding and managing relationships, or taking on a management or leadership role.

ACTIVITY 9

Using the Learning Cycle (Figure 2):

- Review: What are your thoughts and feelings about coaching and mentoring now?

- Learn: What new understandings and insights have you gained from studying this handbook?

- Apply: How might these new understandings and insights inform your practice as a coach/mentor?

SUMMARY

This handbook sets out a clear organisational rationale for higher education establishments which are considering the development of a coaching and/or mentoring scheme. The aim is to examine and support the characteristics of effective professional relationships and working practices.

The handbook offers a number of definitions of coaching and mentoring to clarify, help understanding and inform practices. Definitions are helpful but not sufficient in themselves to inform our practices. This handbook extends our thinking by examining how the practices of coaching and mentoring have explicit links with models of learning. A learning-centred model is introduced to support coaches and mentors in their work.

References

Arnot, J. and Sparrow, J. (2004) *The Coaching Study 2004: Coaching works but it could get better*. Birmingham: Origin and University of Central England.

Bolam, R., McMahon, A., Pocklington, K. and Weindling, D. (1993) *National Evaluation of the Headteacher Mentoring Pilot Schemes*. London: DfES.

Carnell, E. (2000) 'Developing learning-centred professional practice', *Professional Development Today*, 3 (3): 21–32.

Carnell, E. (2001) 'The value of meta-learning dialogue', *Professional Development Today*, 4 (2): 43–54.

Carnell, E. and Lodge, C. (2002) *Supporting Effective Learning*. London: Paul Chapman.

Clutterbuck, D. (1992) *Mentoring*. Henley: Henley Distance Learning.

Cordingly, P., Bell, M. and Temperley, J. (2004) 'Mentoring and coaching: consulting for capacity building'. Unpublished.

Dennison, B. and Kirk, R. (1990) *Do, Review, Learn, Apply: A simple guide to experiential learning*. Oxford: Blackwell.

Daresh, J.C. (1995) 'Research Base on mentoring for educational leaders: what do we know?' *Journal of Educational Administration*, 33 (5): 7–16.

Douglas, C. (1997) *Formal Mentoring Programmes in Organisations: An annotated bibliography*. Greensboro, NC: Centre for Creative Leadership.

Gewirtz, S. (2004) *Taking a Stand: Education policy, sociology and social values*. Inaugural lecture, Thursday 5 February, 2004. Available from: www.kcl.ac.uk/depsta/education/hpages/sgewirtz.html

Grover, K.L. (1994) 'A Study of first year elementary principals and their mentors in the New York City public schools'. Paper presented at the Annual Meeting of the American Research Educational Association, New Orleans, 4–8 April.

Hansford, B., Tennant, L. and Ehrich, L.C. (2002) 'Business mentoring: help or hindrance?' *Mentoring and Tutoring*, 10 (1): 5–20.

Hay, J. (1995) *Transformational Mentoring*. Maidenhead: McGraw-Hill.

Hobson, A. (2003) *Mentoring and Coaching for New Leaders*. Nottingham: National College for School Leadership.

Kay, D. and Hinds, R. (2005) *A Practical Guide to Mentoring*. Oxford: How To Books.

Kolb, D.A. (1984) 'Experiential Learning'. In M. Thorpe, R. Edwards, and A. Hanson (eds), *Culture and Process of Adult Learning*. London: Routledge in association with the Open University.

Little, J.W. (1990) 'The persistence of privacy: autonomy and initiative in teachers' professional relations'. *Teachers' College Record*, 91 (4): 509–36.

Louis, K.S. and Kruse, S.D. (1995) *Professionalism and Community: Perspectives on reforming urban schools*. Thousand Oaks, CA: Sage Publications.

Pennington, R.C. (2004) *Developing Leaders for Today and the Future*. Sheffield: Higher Education Staff Development Agency (HESDA).

Rogers, J. (2004) *Coaching Skills: A handbook*. Milton Keynes: Open University Press.

Sloboda, J. (1986) 'Acquiring Skill.' In A. Gellatly (ed.), *The Skilful Mind: An introduction to cognitive psychology*. Milton Keynes: Open University Press.

Trigwell, K. and Prosser, M. (1996) 'Changing approaches to teaching: a relational perspective'. *Studies in Higher Education*, 21 (3): 275–84.

Watkins, C. (2001) *Learning about Learning enhances Performance*. London: Institute of Education, National School Improvement Network, Research Matters Series No 13.

Watkins, C., Carnell, E., Lodge, C., Wagner, P. and Whalley, C. (1998) *Learning about Learning*. Coventry: NAPCE.

Watkins, C., Carnell, E., Lodge, C., Wagner, P. and Whalley, C. (2002) 'Effective Learning School Improvement Network', *Research Matters*, 17. London: Institute of Education, University of London.

Appendix 1
Support for academic writing and peer support

We report here on two processes that have proved to be very successful at the Institute of Education. The first is the support scheme for academic writing. The second is peer-mentoring groups.

SUPPORT FOR ACADEMIC WRITING

We asked staff who are already benefiting from this provision to say what they felt about the experience. These comments indicate the range of support that is available.

One person felt the individual support helped her build writing into her week making it a regular feature:

Guidance was invaluable to instil a sense of discipline, setting deadlines, planning my time more efficiently around tangible writing projects. Above all, it was ensuring that I kept a space in my busy timetable to commit to writing. It helped me to reflect on my weaknesses, and take steps to address them. And it encouraged me to look above the parapet of the solitary writing pit, and not to be afraid to share the products of my endeavours in seeking the views of others. My confidence has been boosted significantly.

Another highlighted that she was more aware of herself as a writer and used this knowledge to capitalise on positive approaches and limit negative responses:

I benefited from receiving writing support in a number of ways. It was extremely helpful to share with another the obstacles experienced and strategies used when attempting to write. This enabled me to gain an awareness of how I write and the issues involved when trying to write. As a result, my confidence in my abilities has been greatly enhanced because I was able to see the strategies I used as positives rather than negatives. I have been able to reassess what issues are involved for me when I write, from difficulties with getting started to procrastinating with editing final pieces and thus find ways to work with these issues.

One participant identified the importance of scheduling one-to-one sessions in providing continuity:

I have been able to receive practical advice at each stage. In the sessions I work with the facilitator to focus on the task, set goals, share breakthroughs and reflect on barriers I experience.

She goes on to say that the interest and concern of the facilitator helped her to clarify the issues she has with writing.

Overall, receiving writing support has helped me develop my individual skills as a writer sooner, an unexpected bonus from what I initially expected – a one size fits all seminar on writing skills!

Others echo the point that individual needs and concerns are addressed, which is often not possible in group sessions:

Being able to meet several times for shorter periods also allowed for progress to be made and new writing to be discussed at subsequent sessions.

The big advantage is that it is entirely personal and particular to me and my needs. I also feel genuinely free to say what I am thinking, how I feel about it, what my thoughts and ideas are which I know I would probably not do if I was in a group. The sessions are also worked around me and my workload and that makes it easier to manage. I have found it a more positive experience than I was expecting.

All the comments indicate a growing confidence, as this view from a writer with little previous experience shows:

I would highly recommend this provision offered. Since meeting with a writing mentor, my confidence and ability has grown and I feel more comfortable writing within an academic environment.

The learning and teaching and research and consultancy strategies of Higher Education institutions emphasise the need for colleagues to be supported with their writing. At the Institute coaches would work closely within this model with individuals to:

- engage with their interests and motivate and support them
- assist with qualitative analysis, if need be
- read and provide feedback of data and drafts
- free up creativity and strength of voice in the individual.

The individual writer's needs determine the number, length and content of meetings.

PEER MENTORING
GROUPS

A group of staff from across the Institute meets informally as a peer-support group. This is based on a reciprocal peer-led arrangement. Colleagues meet in a small group on a regular basis to support one another to focus on work-related issues. Colleagues taking part in such support networks were asked to report on their views:

I meet with colleagues on a fortnightly basis for one hour. We use the time to give one another support on work-related issues. We have been meeting for two years now and I have found it invaluable. It is the only occasion at work where I have the time to think about my goals and how best to achieve them. This is different than thinking about work on my own. Talking to peers and thinking out loud allows me to articulate issues in a much more conscious and thoughtful way. I'm very lucky to have this opportunity.

It's really important for me to have time in the diary when I can stop and reflect on my job and how it's going. It's also important to do that confidentially with colleagues that I totally trust and whose support I really value. Talking things through as well as listening to them can really help me get a perspective to an issue or concern that I have. Also we all realise we each have things to deal with at work that we feel less alone with.

I look forward to our regular meetings. The dates are put in my diary for each term and I never miss one. The two colleagues in my group are so helpful and very skilled at helping me see my way through any difficulties I encounter. We share the time equally and sometimes we have no problems so it is good just to have the time to review what is going on and makes sense of feelings. I don't ever have the opportunity for this kind of reflection anywhere else. Because we share the time I don't feel I am burdening anyone with my issues. I go away from the meetings uplifted and feel confident that I can deal with any difficulties. Sometimes it is enough just to air them.

Appendix 2
A learning-centred conversation

In coaching and mentoring conversations this model can be applied as a structure when the mentor or coach supports the other person through the different stages:

* reviewing/exploring experiences and issues
* abstracting the learning from this
* exploring possibilities and consequences
* planning the next steps
* being involved in further activity.

A structured approach is one of the main factors in the success of coaching and mentoring schemes (Arnot and Sparrow, 2004).

The conversation may focus on the person's learning, but will be most effective when it also involves an awareness of their learning strategies, blocks to learning, feelings about their learning, the context and their purposes – that is, an understanding of their own learning, or meta-learning. The most effective conversations are explicit about these aspects of learning.

Table 3 outlines a structure to illustrate the stages in a learning conversation, focusing on the review, learn and apply aspects of the learning cycle. The skills used by the coach and mentor have been identified. Some examples of prompts to help the conversation along are included. (For specific coaching/mentoring questions see Appendix 3.)

The example prompts included in this table are non-specific. For that reason they may look more sophisticated than they might be in practice as prompts at the 'learning stage' connect with what emerges from the 'reviewing stage' of the conversation. The language may be unfamiliar. But when it is related to content it becomes more accessible. For learning to be effective language needs to become richer as this will extend the mentee's/coachee's thinking and understanding. (For specific coaching/mentoring questions see Appendix 3.)

THE COACH'S/ MENTOR'S ROLE

The role is to structure the learning conversation by moving the other person through the stages; the order of prompts encourages this. The structure ensures reflection on the activity at the outset, moving on to learning from the experiences, planning future action and strategies and finally reflecting at a meta-learning level. In this way the conversation follows a complete cycle of learning. This cycle may not be completed in a single session. It may take several sessions. In addition, the cycle may not be completed in this order, but the conversation may go backwards and forwards between stages before progressing to the final stages.

TABLE 3 Stages of learning conversation skills for coaches/mentors

Stages of learning conversation	Skills for coaches/mentors	Examples of prompts
• Reviewing Exploring the situation	• active listening • asking open questions • being non-judgemental • summarising	What's happening? What's going well? And not so well... How do you feel about this?
• Learning Identifying new insights and understanding	• empathising • reflecting back • sharing insights	How do you make sense of what's happening? New insights you have gained are... * Are you noticing any patterns in your learning? What have you noticed about what helps your learning and what blocks it? It seems as if...
• Applying Taking the learning forward	• establish clear, negotiated goals • planning and identifying next stages	Your next steps will be..? * What and who do you need to help you? If you get stuck you will talk to..? * When will the next review be most helpful?
• Review of the learning conversation This is a meta-learning level. Its purpose is to stand back from the conversation and consider how it helped or hindered learning	Skills at this stage are the same as those in the earlier review stage: • active listening • asking open questions • being non-judgmental • summarising	What did you notice about today's session? In what ways did you find it effective? How would you describe the changes in your feelings during the session? In what ways are you finding talking about your learning more effective? Is there anything you are noticing about my role that is helping or hindering your learning?

* The coach/mentor does not complete this sentence but encourages the other person to do so. It is a prompt.

There are some important points to note about the conversation. For example, questions and prompts should be open-ended and invite exploration, as relentless questioning can be off-putting. There should be time to allow for thinking and there may be some periods of silence.

The coach/mentor may not be the main source of ideas for future strategies so the coachee/mentee can be encouraged to:

- **Use his or her imagination:**
  for example, *what might you do? What might a friend advise you to do?*

- **Think of other credible people:**
  for example, *do you know of anyone who seems to be handling this sort of issue well? What might X do?*

- **Think as a third party:**
  for example, *if you were advising a friend about this, what could help them?*

- **Anticipate:**
  for example, *what will help me succeed or hinder me? How might others respond?* (Watkins and Butcher, 1995)

Helping someone review their progress and achievement requires the skills of active listening and appropriate questioning or prompting. Active listening requires respect, sincerity and genuineness. It involves paraphrasing, prompting and probing. It needs judgement about the use of open, closed and leading questions and when to move forward. Although the coach/mentor often speaks very little, they will be concentrating hard on listening, checking their physical responses, monitoring the progress of the review and deciding when to move on.

The other person's contributions grow as they develop a shared language with which to describe their learning through talking about learning with each other.

Appendix 3
Examples of coaching/mentoring questions

- What is the issue you wish to discuss?

- What makes it an issue now?

- Whose issue/problem is it?

- How important is it?

- What have you tried so far?

- Imagine this issue is resolved. What would you see, hear and feel?

- What is standing in the way of the ideal outcome?

- What is your responsibility for what has been happening?

- Has anything like this happened before?

- What are early signs that things might be improving?

- Imagine you are at your most resourceful. What do you say to yourself about this issue?

- What are the options for action here?

- What criteria would you use to judge these options?

- Which option seems best against the criteria?

- What is the next best step?

- When will you take it?

(Adapted from Rogers 2004: 65)

Appendix 4
Evaluation of the scheme: questions for the coach/mentor

1. To what extent did the initial guidelines/briefings regarding the coaching/mentoring scheme assist your orientation to the process?

2. Please indicate the number of meetings you have had.

3. How would you rate the overall effectiveness of the meetings you have had?

4. Describe the most significant themes/issues that emerged from the meetings.

5. Describe your feelings about the meetings. In what ways can you detect that your feelings changed over the period of the meetings. How can you account for this?

6. What new insights and understandings have you gained from the process of coaching and mentoring?

7. What changes have come about as a result of the process?

8. Have there been other, unintended or wider benefits that have emerged during your coaching/mentoring relationship and meetings?

9. What factors contributed to making the coaching/mentoring relationship and meetings successful?

10. What factors hindered success?

11. Other thoughts you may have ...

12. What changes would you suggest to the scheme?

(Developed from Pennington, 2004)

Appendix 5
Evaluation of the scheme: questions for the mentee/coachee

1. To what extent did the initial guidelines/briefings regarding the coaching/mentoring scheme assist your orientation to the process?

2. Please indicate the number of meetings you have had. What is your view about the optimal frequency/timings of meetings to ensure effectiveness?

3. How would you rate the overall effectiveness of the meetings you have had?

4. Describe the most significant themes/issues that emerged from the meetings.

5. Describe your feelings about the meetings. In what ways can you detect that your feelings changed over the period of the meetings? How can you account for this?

6. What new insights and understandings have you gained from the process of coaching and mentoring?

7. What changes have come about as a result of the process?

8. Have there been other, unintended or wider benefits that have emerged during your coaching/mentoring relationship and meetings?

9. What factors contributed to making the coaching/mentoring relationship and meetings successful?

10. What factors hindered success?

11. Other thoughts you may have ...

12. What changes would you suggest to the scheme?

(Developed from Pennington, 2004)